The Garden Year

January brings the snow,
Makes our feet and fingers glow.

February brings the rain,
Thaws the frozen lake again.

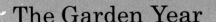

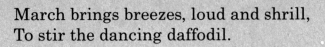

March brings breezes, loud and shrill,
To stir the dancing daffodil.

April brings the primrose sweet,
Scatters daisies at our feet.

May brings flocks of pretty lambs,
Skipping by their fleecy dams.

June brings tulips, lilies, roses,
Fills the children's hands with posies.

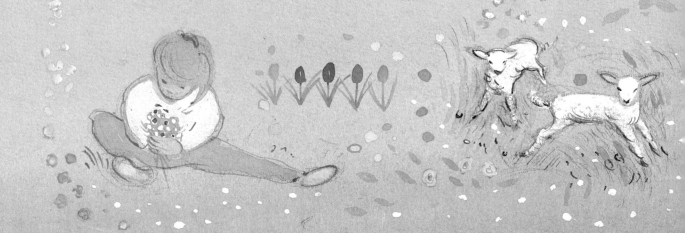

Hot July brings cooling showers,
Apricots and gillyflowers.

August brings the sheaves of corn,
Then the harvest home is borne.

Warm September brings the fruit;
Sportsmen then begin to shoot.

Fresh October brings the pheasant;
Then to gather nuts is pleasant.

Dull November brings the blast;
Then the leaves are whirling fast.

Chill December brings the sleet,
Blazing fire, and Christmas treat.

Sara Coleridge

The Twelve Months

Snowy, Flowy, Blowy,
Showery, Flowery, Bowery,
Hoppy, Croppy, Droppy,
Breezy, Sneezy, Freezy.

Anon.

Oxford University Press, Great Clarendon Street, Oxford OX2 6DP

Oxford is a trade mark of Oxford University Press

Original text material copyright © Vince Cross 1997
Illustrations copyright © Robin Bell Corfield 1997
This selection and arrangement copyright © Vince Cross 1997
First published 1997

Vince Cross and Robin Bell Corfield have asserted their moral right to be
identified as the authors of this work.

'The Song of the Weather' by Michael Flanders is
reprinted by kind permission of Mrs Claudia Flanders.

A CIP catalogue record for this book is available
from the British Library

ISBN 0 19 276067 X (hardback)
ISBN 0 19 276070 X (paperback)

Printed at Oriental Press, Dubai, U.A.E.

ALL THE YEAR ROUND

POEMS THROUGH THE SEASONS

Written and selected by Vince Cross

Illustrated by Robin Bell Corfield

Oxford University Press

Welcome with a wish
This bonny New Year
What it may bring
Will shortly appear . . .

More joy than pain
More promise than fear
So make good your wish
For this bonny New Year.

A Cherry Year

A cherry year,
A merry year;
A pear year,
A dear year;
A plum year,
A dumb year.

Traditional

St Valentine's Day

Good morrow to you, Valentine.
Curl your locks as I do mine,
Two before and three behind.
Good morrow to you, Valentine.

Traditional

Mother's Day

My mum's special,
The only one.
No one like her
Under the sun.
So just for today,
A present from me,
Breakfast in bed.
Buttered toast and tea.

Vince Cross

Easter Hurrah

Let's dance for Easter
and everything's new.
A lick of spring paint
tree green, sky blue,
makes hope leap high
as dreary days
are danced away
in an Easter praise.

Vince Cross

Sweet Spring

The trees are clouds of coconut-ice,
The air is peppermint bright.
The fields are terrines of browns and greens
In the morning's milky light.

The hedges and paths are spread with sweets,
Primroses preserved in dew.
The spider's run is sugar spun
As a master chef might do.

The drifts of grass are apple mousse,
Wild honey in the may.
Everything scrumptious, good and delicious
For you this fresh spring day.

Vince Cross

May Day

It's cold and wet, the skies are grey,
The weather you'd expect on the first of May,
And down the street, you can catch the sound,
Of a morris band in the school playground.

Under the umbrellas, beneath the trees,
Bedraggled dancers stand and freeze,
And stand and freeze, and wait their chance,
For a twisting, turning, maypole dance.

One to a ribbon, red, white and blue,
They never remember what to do,
Looking at each other with a nervous glance,
Oh, how do we untangle this maypole dance?

The sun comes out, the band plays on,
Verse after verse of the maypole song,
Till the strings unwind and the dancers advance.
Give three cheers for the maypole dance!

Vince Cross

Swarms

A swarm of bees in May,
Is worth a load of hay.
A swarm of bees in June,
Is worth a silver spoon.
A swarm of bees in July,
Is not worth a fly.

Traditional

Summer

Winter is cold-hearted,
Spring is yea and nay,
Autumn is a weathercock,
Blown every way.
Summer days for me,
When every leaf is on its tree.

Christina Rossetti

Rosebud in June

It's a rosebud in June
And the violets in bloom.
And small birds are singing
Love songs on each spray.
We'll pipe and we'll sing, love,
We'll dance in a ring, love,
Each lad with his lass,
All on the green grass.
And it's all to plough
Where the oxen graze low,
And the lads and their lasses
Do sheep-shearing go.

Traditional

My Holiday

You'll like it when we get there,
My dad said to me,
Only another half an hour,
And you'll catch a glimpse of the sea.

Isn't it lovely on the beach,
My mum said to me.
I'm sure it'll brighten up a bit
If we brew a pot of tea.

You'll really enjoy the funfair,
Big brother said to me.
You'll not be sick like last time,
No chance, at least, you might not be.

Why are you always reading books?
My sister said to me.
Let's go and look at the old wooden pier.
There's a boy up there I fancy.

Aren't you enjoying your holiday?
My family said to me.
No, I thought, I'd rather be back
With my toys and my TV.

Honest, I did enjoy it,
I said to my family,
It was being with you that mattered most,
Not being at the sea.

Vince Cross

Harvest Fayre

The label on the box
Says 'Handle with care',
Inside is my gift
For the Harvest Fayre.

There are green and juicy
Apples from our trees.
I picked them with Dad.
He gave me these.

There are plump and glistening
Blackberries from the briars
At the end of the scrapyard
Behind the old tyres.

There are delicate and perfumed
Teas in a pack.
Mum had them for Christmas,
A year or two back.

But to me, best of all
Are my long runner beans.
I've watched them grow,
You don't know what it means

That I can see them there
High on display.
My own bit of harvest on this
Thank you day.

Vince Cross

Autumn Fires

In the other gardens
And all up the vale,
From the autumn bonfires
See the smoke trail!

Pleasant summer over
And all the summer flowers,
The red fire blazes,
The grey smoke towers.

Sing a song of seasons!
Something bright in all!
Flowers in the summer,
Fires in the fall!

Robert Louis Stevenson

Warm Hands

Warm hands, warm,
The men are gone to plough,
If you want to warm your hands,
Warm your hands now.

Traditional

Fun at Hallowe'en

Have you got the message, kid?
Then don't do what I did.
Forget trick or treat
In our street.

I was pelted with stale bread,
Got water on my head.
They're really not that keen
On Hallowe'en.

There's nothing to be done
On October thirty-one,
So stay at home and try
Pumpkin pie.
Ugh!
Have another try at liking
Pumpkin pie.

Vince Cross

Guy Fawkes

Remember, remember
The fifth of November,
Gunpowder, treason and plot;
I see no reason
Why gunpowder treason
Should ever be forgot.

Traditional

Winter Wise

Walk fast in snow, in frost walk slow,
And still as you go, tread on your toe.
When frost and snow are both together,
Sit by the fire, and spare shoe leather.

Anon.

Three Children Sliding on the Ice

Three children sliding on the ice,
All on a winter's day.
As it fell out, they all fell in,
The rest they ran away.

Now had these children been at home
Or sliding on dry ground,
Ten thousand pounds to one penny
They had not all been drowned.

You parents all that children have
And you that have got none,
If you would keep them safe abroad,
Pray keep them safe at home!

Traditional

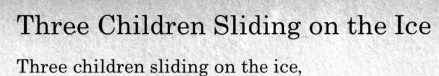

Christmas is coming

Christmas is coming,
The goose is getting fat,
Please to put a penny
In the old man's hat.
If you haven't got a penny
A ha'penny will do.
If you haven't got a ha'penny,
God bless you!

Traditional

Candles

I like to set a candle
Dancing in the dark,
So shadows loom around the room
From its tiny spark.

If I could make a candle
Sleek and shiny red,
Its melting form would keep me warm
Each night beside my bed.

Candles are for Hanukkah,
And for Diwali too,
The welcoming light of Christmas night,
Blessing me and you.

Vince Cross

Auld Lang Syne

Should auld acquaintance be forgot
And never brought to mind?
Should auld acquaintance be forgot
And days of auld lang syne?

And here's a hand, my trusty friend,
And gie's a hand o'thine;
We'll take a cup of kindness yet
For auld lang syne.

For auld lang syne, my dear,
For auld lang syne,
We'll take a cup of kindness yet
For the sake of auld lang syne.

Robert Burns

Hail and Farewell

Sing reign of Fair Maid
With gold upon her toe,
Open you the West Door
And turn the Old Year go.

Sing reign of Fair Maid
With gold upon her chin,
Open you the East Door
And let the New Year in.

Unknown

The Song of the Weather

January brings the snow
Makes your feet and fingers glow.

February's ice and sleet
Freeze the toes right off your feet.

Welcome March with wintry wind
Would thou wert not so unkind.

April brings the sweet spring showers
On and on for hours and hours.

Farmers fear unkindly May
Frost by night and hail by day.

June just rains and never stops
For thirty days and spoils the crops.

In July the sun is hot.
Is it shining? No, it's not.

August cold and dank and wet
Brings more rain than any yet.

Bleak September's mist and mud
Is enough to chill the blood.

Then October adds a gale
Wind and slush and rain and hail.

Dark November brings the fog
Shouldn't do it to a dog.

Freezing, wet, December, then . . .
Dear old January again!

Michael Flanders